Two-Hour Cross-Stitch

Two-Hour Cross-Stitch

515 Fabulous Designs

Patrice Boerens

A STERLING/CHAPELLE BOOK
Sterling Publishing Co. Inc.   New York

Library of Congress Cataloging-in Publication Data Available

Boerens, Patrice.
    Two-hour cross-stitch : 515 fabulous designs / Patrice Boerens.
        p.   cm.
    "A Sterling/Chapelle book."
    Includes index.
    ISBN 0-8069-0952-8
    1. Cross-stitch—Patterns. 2. Decoration and ornament—Victorian
style. 3. Nature in art. 4. Children in art. I. Title.
TT778.C76B64   1994
746. 44'3 041—dc20   94-30301
                                                      CIP

10 9 8 7 6 5 4 3
Published by Sterling Publishing Company, Inc.
387 Park Avenue South, New York, N.Y. 10016
© 1994 by Chapelle Ltd.
Distributed in Canada by Sterling Publishing
℅ Canadian Manda Group, P.O. Box 920, Station U
Toronto, Ontario, Canada M8Z 5P9
Distributed in Great Britain and Europe by Cassell PLC
Villiers House, 41/47 Strand, London WC2N 5JE, England
Distributed in Australia by Capricorn Link (Australia) Pty Ltd.
P.O.Box 6651, Baulkham Hills, Business Center, NSW 2153, Australia
Printed and bound in Hong Kong
All Rights Reserved

Sterling ISBN 0-8069-0952-8

For Chapelle Ltd.

Owner

Jo Packham

Staff

Patrice Boerens

Gaylene Byers

Rebecca Christensen

Holly Fuller

Cherie Hanson

Holly Hollingsworth

Susan Jorgensen

Lorin May

Florence Stacey

Nancy Whitley

Lorrie Young

Photography

Ryne Hazen

INTRODUCTION

 f you've stitched creations from The Vanessa-Ann Collection or just browsed through their books and leaflets, you've become familiar with the artistic works of designer Patrice Liljenquist Boerens. A graduate in graphic arts from Brigham Young University, Patrice has been designing for The Vanessa-Ann Collection for over 13 years.

She is a native of Ogden, Utah, where she lives with her husband and four children. She works in numerous artistic mediums, including water-color, colored pencil, ink, wood, and fabric.

CONTENTS

chapter one

NATURE

*In his garden every man may
be his own artist without
apology or explanation.
Here is one spot where each
may experience the
"romance of possibility."*

-Louise Beebe Wilder

Step 1: Cross-stitch (2 strands)

DMC

−	725
∴	721
●	347
△	327
✕	334
□	562
▲	839

Step 2: Backstitch (1 strand)

⌐ 310

Step 1: Cross-stitch (2 strands)

DMC

■	729
○	352
+	347
△	327
✕	334
∴	562
✎	435

Step 2: Backstitch (1 strand)

⌐ 310

Step 3: French Knot (1 strand)

● 310

❧ *Nature 11*

Step 1: Cross-stitch (2 strands)

DMC

	725
×	3687
○	326
▲	327
□	334
∴	562
●	611

Step 2: Backstitch (1 strand)

⌐ 310

Step 3: French Knot (1 strand)

✦ 310

Step 1: Cross-stitch (2 strands)
       DMC

●	335
✕	326
∴	334
□	992
■	991

❖ *Nature 13*

Step 1: Cross-stitch (2 strands)

DMC

⊺		3716
○		351
✕		341
●		3746
△		334
∴		988
■		986
▲		3799

Step 2: Backstitch (1 strand)

⌐	3799

❧ Nature 15

Step 1: Cross-stitch (2 strands)

DMC

+	745
○	352
●	350
✕	340
△	913
∴	910
☐	840
■	839

Step 2: Backstitch (1 strand)

⌐	350

Step 1: Cross-stitch (2 strands)

926	│		Ecru
301	○	744	Yellow-pale
328	X	3341	Apricot
332	■	946	Burnt Orange-med.
47	∴	321	Christmas Red

246	●	895	Christmas Green-dk.
357	△	801	Coffee Brown-dk.
403	╱	310	Black

Step 2: Backstitch (1 strand)

246		895	Christmas Green-dk. (flower)
357		801	Coffee Brown-dk. (rooster)
403		310	Black (all else)

Step 3: French Knot (1 strand)

357	▸	801	Coffee Brown-dk.
403	●	310	Black

⊰ *Nature 17*

Step 1: Cross-stitch (2 strands)

DMC

■	3341
●	603
∴	327
○	799
□	798
△	369
✕	991
▲	3772

Step 2: Backstitch (1 strand)

⌐	603

Step 1: Cross-stitch (2 strands)

DMC

∣	744	
○	760	
∴	347	
□	211	
✕	210	
▲	208	
△	704	
■	701	

Step 2: Backstitch (1 strand)

⌐ 208

☙ *Nature 19*

Step 1: Cross-stitch (2 strands)

DMC

	977
○	356
●	355
✕	327
∴	3768
△	987
✗	936
■	3799

Step 2: Backstitch (1 strand)

└ 3799

Step 1: Cross-stitch (2 strands)

DMC

✕	402
❘	353
○	352
△	554
▲	552
☐	3347
∴	3345
●	3781

Step 2: Backstitch (1 strand)

⌐	353
⌐	3781

Step 1: Cross-stitch (2 strands)

DMC

○   727
●   725
+   776
✕   800
□   793
■   792
◇   3781
▲   3799

Step 2: Backstitch (1 strand)

⌐   3781
⌐   3799

Good Morning Sunshine

Good Evening Moon

Step 1: Cross-stitch (2 strands)

DMC

ǀ	3688
△	3687
∴	554
○	800
✕	966
▢	563
●	561

Step 2: Backstitch (1 strand)

⌐ 844

ᵗ♣ *Nature 23*

Step 1: Cross-stitch (2 strands)

DMC

○	725
▲	729
–	224
■	518
+	734
∴	469
✕	632
●	310

Step 2: Backstitch (1 strand)

⌐	632
⌐	310

Step 3: French Knot (1 strand)

◆	310

Step 1: Cross-stitch (2 strands)

DMC

○	676
●	729
+	402
△	3687
▲	3685
✕	553
■	986
∴	3787

Step 2: Backstitch (1 strand)

	986
	3787

Nature 25

Step 1: Cross-stitch (2 strands)

DMC

○	725
△	3712
●	350
✕	327
+	793
□	913
∴	910
▲	500

Step 2: Backstitch (1 strand)

⌐	913
⌐	500

Step 1: Cross-stitch (2 strands)

DMC

+	**725**
∴	**722**
○	**900**
●	**817**
✕	**3347**
△	**3346**
▲	**986**

Step 2: Backstitch (1 strand)

⌐	**3799**

☙ *Nature 27*

Step 1: Cross-stitch (2 strands)

DMC

−	**744**
+	**353**
○	**352**
●	**350**
✕	**334**
□	**992**
■	**991**
◇	**3781**

Step 2: Backstitch (1 strand)

∟	**3781**

Step 1: Cross-stitch (2 strands)

DMC

	676
○	402
△	961
▲	3685
∴	209
□	966
✕	562

Step 2: Backstitch (1 strand)

⌐ 562

⌐ 3371

Step 1: Cross-stitch (2 strands)

DMC

ꞁ	Ecru
○	422
∕	407
●	632
·	3782
□	640
✕	3031

Step 2: Backstitch (1 strand)

⌐	3371

Step 3: French Knot (1 strand)

◆	3371

Step 1: Cross-stitch (2 strands)

DMC

●	327
✕	407
+	632
□	3031
○	640
■	844

Step 2: Backstitch (1 strand)

⌐ 3371

Step 1: Cross-stitch (2 strands)

DMC

−	White
✕	729
□	722
∴	3347
▲	3362
○	400
△	3022
●	3021

Step 2: Backstitch (1 strand)

3021

Step 1: Cross-stitch (2 strands)

DMC

+	727
∴	725
□	783
✗	722
▲	3362
△	890
○	434
●	938

Step 2: Backstitch (1 strand)

⌐	434
⌐	938

✤ *Nature 33*

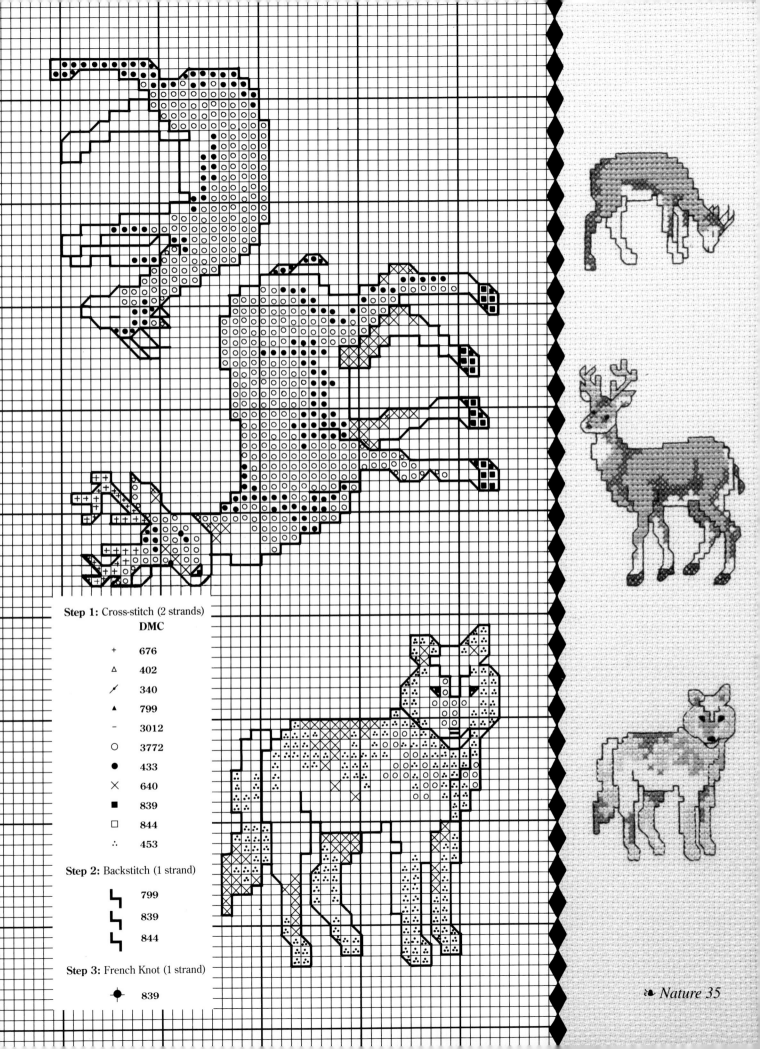

Step 1: Cross-stitch (2 strands)

DMC

+	676
△	402
✕	340
▲	799
−	3012
○	3772
●	433
✕	640
■	839
□	844
∴	453

Step 2: Backstitch (1 strand)

⌐	799
⌐	839
⌐	844

Step 3: French Knot (1 strand)

●	839

Step 1: Cross-stitch (2 strands)

DMC

○	725
Ɩ	353
∴	722
✕	3755
▲	989
□	839
●	310

Step 2: Backstitch (1 strand)

⌐	310

Step 1: Cross-stitch (2 strands)

DMC

○ 725
▲ 722
∴ 3755
■ 322
╱ 986
+ 3782
□ 839

Step 2: Backstitch (1 strand)

⌐ 310

Step 1: Cross-stitch (2 strands)

DMC

- − 722
- ✕ 720
- ∴ 327
- ○ 3755
- ● 312
- ▲ 3750
- △ 992

Step 2: Backstitch (1 strand)

327

3750

Step 3: French Knot (1 strand)

◆ 3750

Step 1: Cross-stitch (2 strands)

DMC

	353
O	326
✗	211
∴	327
✕	334
▲	959
□	955

Step 2: Backstitch (1 strand)

⌐ 310

chapter two

CHILDREN

*A babe in a house is a
well-spring of pleasure, a
messenger of peace and love,
a resting-place for innocence
on earth; a link between
angels and men.*

-M.F. Tupper

Step 1: Cross-stitch (2 strands)

DMC

∣	676
○	335
✕	326
╱	340
●	327
∴	564
□	433
▲	310

Step 2: Backstitch (1 strand)

⌐	310

Step 3: French Knot (1 strand)

✦	310

Step 1: Cross-stitch (2 strands)

DMC

		743
△		922
●		326
∴		809
✕		958
○		436
✁		433

Step 2: Backstitch (1 strand)

⌐ 310

Step 3: French Knot (1 strand)

◆ 310

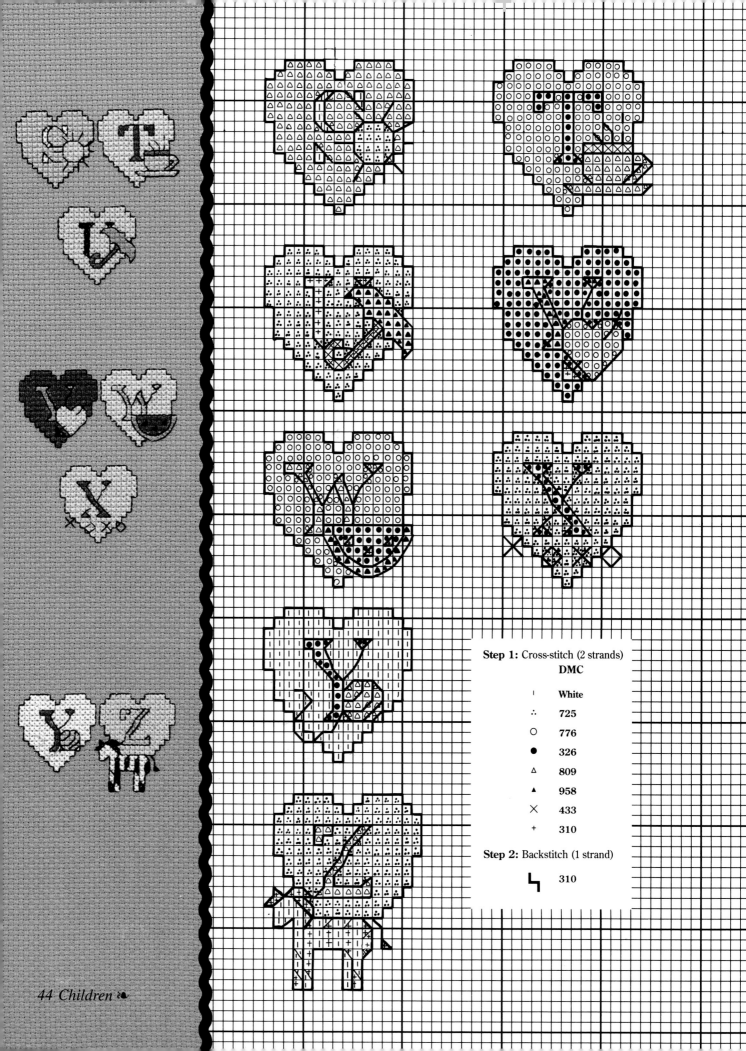

Step 1: Cross-stitch (2 strands)
DMC

ǀ	White
∴	725
○	776
●	326
△	809
▲	958
✕	433
+	310

Step 2: Backstitch (1 strand)

⌐ 310

44 Children

Step 1: Cross-stitch (2 strands)

DMC

+	963
○	962
●	3350
×	340
▲	824
□	959
■	434

Step 2: Backstitch (1 strand)

⌐ 3750

Step 1: Cross-stitch (2 strands)

DMC

ı	725
○	722
×	347
∴	553
·	813
●	825
△	993

Step 2: Backstitch (1 strand)

⌐ 310

Step 3: French Knot (1 strand)

⬥ 310

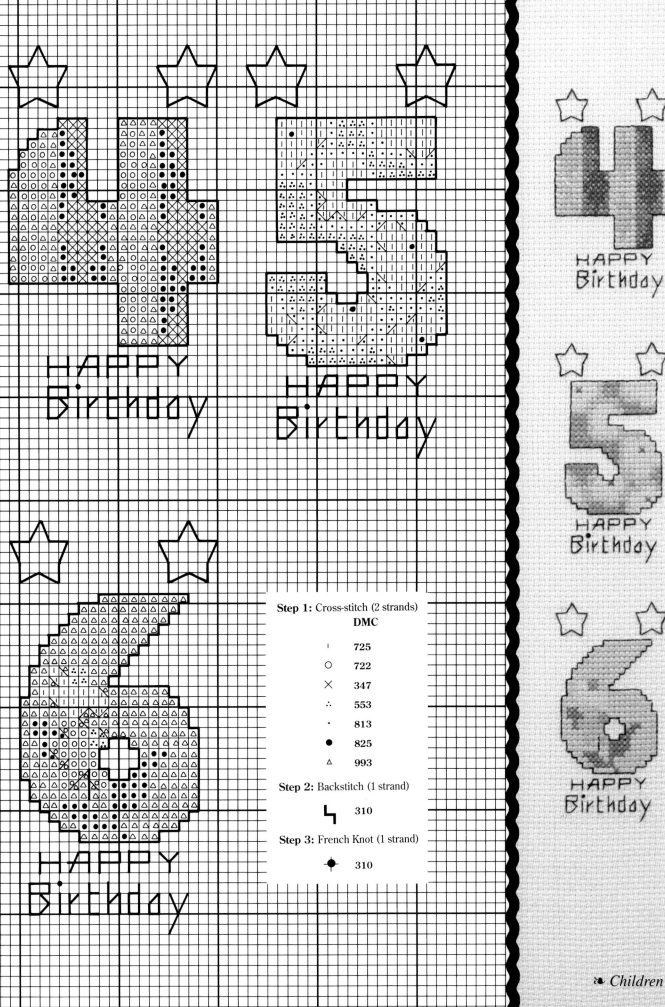

Step 1: Cross-stitch (2 strands)

DMC

I	725
○	722
✕	347
∴	553
·	813
●	825
△	993

Step 2: Backstitch (1 strand)

⌐	310

Step 3: French Knot (1 strand)

●	310

Step 1: Cross-stitch (2 strands)

DMC

I	725
O	722
X	347
∴	553
·	813
●	825
△	993

Step 2: Backstitch (1 strand)

└ 310

Step 3: French Knot (1 strand)

● 310

Step 1: Cross-stitch (2 strands)

DMC

○	972
+	760
●	321
✕	550
■	334
△	368
∴	319
╱	433

Step 2: Backstitch (1 strand)

⌐	550
⌐	368

Children 49

Step 1: Cross-stitch (2 strands)

DMC

+	727
○	3354
●	3350
×	3746
□	827
◇	993
■	991

Step 2: Backstitch (1 strand)

⌐ 311

Step 3: French Knot (1 strand)

◆ 311

Step 1: Cross-stitch (2 strands)

DMC

○	745
●	743
△	3328
∴	347
✕	813
■	824
+	954
□	839

Step 2: Backstitch (1 strand)

⌐ 839

Step 3: French Knot (1 strand)

● 839

Step 1: Cross-stitch (2 strands)

DMC

+	746
○	677
●	676
□	963
■	962
✕	3766
·	840
◇	310

Step 2: Backstitch (1 strand)

⌐	310

Step 3: French Knot (1 strand)

✦	310

Step 1: Cross-stitch (2 strands)

DMC

−	3078
▲	3776
○	899
╱	341
∴	334
□	564
■	562
✕	841
●	3799

Step 2: Backstitch (1 strand)

⌐	3776
⌐	3799

♣ Children 53

Step 1: Cross-stitch (2 strands)

DMC

·	White
○	349
×	210
+	3325
●	796
△	993
□	436
■	310

Step 2: Backstitch (1 strand)

⌐	796
⌐	436

Step 1: Cross-stitch (2 strands)

DMC

○	**326**
∴	**815**
✕	**793**
✗	**792**
□	**954**
−	**739**
△	**839**
●	**310**

Step 2: Backstitch (1 strand)

⌐ **310**

Step 3: French Knot (1 strand)

● **310**

○ 352
✕ 309
● 304
+ 813
∴ 825
□ 992
△ 991
■ 3787

Step 2: Backstitch (1 strand)

⌐ 825

Step 1: Cross-stitch (2 strands)

DMC

−	**725**
○	**729**
●	**816**
∴	**340**
×	**327**
╱	**334**
△	**3347**
+	**3362**

Step 2: Backstitch (1 strand)

⌐ **3362**

Step 1: Cross-stitch (2 strands)

DMC

○	3047
∴	335
●	327
△	3752
▲	826
I	966
✕	992
╱	841

Step 2: Backstitch (1 strand)

⌐ 327

Step 1: Cross-stitch (2 strands)

DMC

□	745
○	776
◇	3731
△	340
✕	333
●	597
+	966
■	562

Step 2: Backstitch (1 strand)

⌐	333

Step 1: Cross-stitch (2 strands)
DMC

−	3770
○	743
∴	722
✕	961
●	553
△	322
□	3347
■	938

Step 2: Backstitch (1 strand)

⌐	961
⌐	553
⌐	938

Step 3: French Knot (1 strand)

◆	3347
◆	938

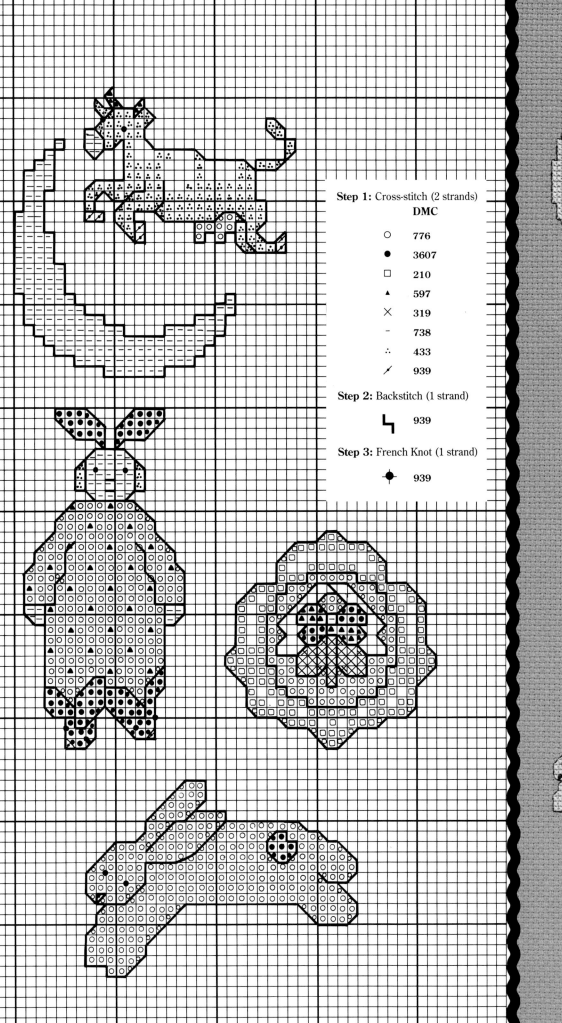

Step 1: Cross-stitch (2 strands)

DMC

○	776
●	3607
□	210
▲	597
✕	319
−	738
∴	433
✧	939

Step 2: Backstitch (1 strand)

┐ 939

Step 3: French Knot (1 strand)

● 939

Step 1: Cross-stitch (2 strands)
DMC

-	**729**
▲	**3733**
△	**326**
✗	**327**
■	**336**
∴	**993**
●	**991**
○	**3021**

Step 2: Backstitch (1 strand)

⌐	**327**
⌐	**991**
⌐	**3021**

Step 3: French Knot (1 strand)

◆	**3021**

Step 1: Cross-stitch (2 strands)

DMC

+	White
○	742
×	352
●	321
∴	807
△	368
⁄	561
▲	310

Step 2: Backstitch (1 strand)

⌐	321
⌐	310

Step 1: Cross-stitch (2 strands)

DMC

+	**743**
○	**721**
◇	**3716**
×	**327**
●	**519**
◆	**3363**
□	**433**
■	**310**

Step 2: Backstitch (1 strand)

⌐	**327**
⌐	**310**

Step 3: French Knot (1 strand)

✦	**310**

Step 1: Cross-stitch (2 strands)

DMC

○   761

✕   351

△   210

▲   208

∴   311

□   320

−   543

●   310

Step 2: Backstitch (1 strand)

⌐   310

Step 3: French Knot (1 strand)

●   310

🖙 *Children 65*

Step 1: Cross-stitch (2 strands)

DMC

+	725
□	352
○	605
▲	326
∴	552
∕	809
✕	806
●	3799

Step 2: Backstitch (1 strand)

⌐	3799

Step 1: Cross-stitch (2 strands)
DMC

+	3341
×	776
●	335
□	554
∴	550
／	564
▲	422
○	762

Step 2: Backstitch (1 strand)

⌐ 550

Step 3: French Knot (1 strand)

● 550

Step 1: Cross-stitch (2 strands)

DMC

−	445
∴	973
△	335
▲	326
+	3755
○	986
✕	3064
●	844

Step 2: Backstitch (1 strand)

⌐	844

Step 1: Cross-stitch (2 strands)

DMC

+	225
●	899
△	3752
▲	322
✦	989
○	975
∴	317
□	310

Step 2: Backstitch (1 strand)

⌐ 310

Step 3: French Knot (1 strand)

◆ 310

Step 1: Cross-stitch (2 strands)

DMC

+	Ecru
I	738
✕	437
□	3790
○	632
▲	844
●	310

Step 2: Backstitch (1 strand)

⌐	938
⌐	310

Step 3: French Knot (1 strand)

✦	938

Step 1: Cross-stitch (2 strands)

DMC

∣	744
○	326
╱	209
∴	959
✕	322
△	3772
▲	632
+	3799

Step 2: Backstitch (1 strand)

⌐ 3799

Step 3: French Knot (1 strand)

◆ 3799

Step 1: Cross-stitch (2 strands)
DMC

○ 725
· 945
✕ 977
■ 349
+ 3753
● 791
□ 869

Step 2: Backstitch (1 strand)

∟ 310

Step 3: French Knot (1 strand)

✦ 310

Step 1: Cross-stitch (2 strands)
DMC

□	725
△	722
✕	976
∴	347
▲	322
·	3772
○	632
●	938

Step 2: Backstitch (1 strand)

⌐ 347

⌐ 938

Step 3: French Knot (1 strand)

● 938

Step 4: Buttons

■

Step 1: Cross-stitch (2 strands)

DMC

| | 676
○ 402
▲ 351
✗ 518
● 792
✕ 367
∴ 3772
△ 3371

Step 2: Backstitch (1 strand)

⌐ 3371

Step 3: French Knot (1 strand)

◆ 3371

Step 1: Cross-stitch (2 strands)

DMC

○	725
✕	351
△	335
∴	326
●	553
╱	792
ı	964

Step 2: Backstitch (1 strand)

⌐ 823

Step 3: French Knot (1 strand)

● 823

Step 1: Cross-stitch (2 strands)

DMC

■	3687
◇	902
+	3750
○	400
✕	611
□	632
●	844

Step 2: Backstitch (1 strand)

⌐	3799

Step 3: French Knot (1 strand)

●	3799

Children 77

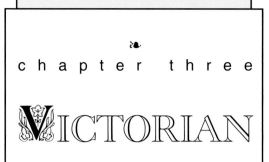

VICTORIAN

Happy in our love to-day,
Light as air we sail away,
To my heart you hold the key,
For you're all the world to me.

-Unknown

Step 1: Cross-stitch (2 strands)

DMC

○	**760**
∴	**3328**
✁	**3685**
●	**327**
△	**3755**
✕	**368**
■	**987**

Step 2: Backstitch (1 strand)

⌐	**310**

Step 1: Cross-stitch (2 strands)

DMC

+	760
○	3328
●	3731
◇	3685
✕	518
∴	989
□	986

Step 2: Backstitch (1 strand)

⌐ 310

Step 3: French Knot (1 strand)

● 310

Step 1: Cross-stitch (2 strands)

DMC

○ 676

∴ 3328

■ 816

△ 3325

╱ 927

✕ 993

● 936

Step 2: Backstitch (1 strand)

└ 310

Step 1: Cross-stitch (2 strands)

DMC

+	Ecru
○	760
■	930
×	992
∴	991
●	3778
✗	738

Step 2: Backstitch (1 strand)

⌐	310

Victorian 83

Step 1: Cross-stitch (2 strands)

DMC

+	3046
o	3776
▲	921
∴	816
□	3042
●	327
✕	320

Step 2: Backstitch (1 strand)

⌐ 310

Step 1: Cross-stitch (2 strands)

DMC

+	676
○	760
●	3328
╱	221
∴	3740
✕	3364
□	987

Step 2: Backstitch (1 strand)

⌐ 310

Step 3: French Knot (1 strand)

◆ 310

Step 1: Cross-stitch (2 strands)

DMC

+	3779
●	920
✕	3740
△	3364
○	3768
■	991
□	452

Step 2: Backstitch (1 strand)

⌐	310

Step 1: Cross-stitch (2 strands)

DMC

+	**676**
□	**3712**
×	**3350**
○	**315**
●	**3685**
△	**806**
⟋	**730**

Step 2: Backstitch (1 strand)

⌐	**310**

Step 1: Cross-stitch (2 strands)

DMC

○	976
●	3777
✕	3041
△	793
□	806
∴	500
+	437

Step 2: Backstitch (1 strand)

⌐	310

Step 1: Cross-stitch (2 strands)

DMC

+	761
∴	3712
▲	347
△	554
■	553
○	320
✕	992
●	991

Step 2: Backstitch (1 strand)

⌐	347

Step 1: Cross-stitch (2 strands)

DMC

·	Ecru
○	353
□	211
▲	209
−	775
●	3755
✕	840
∴	3799

Step 2: Backstitch (1 strand)

⌐	3799

Step 1: Cross-stitch (2 strands)

DMC

+	676
◇	725
■	782
○	3688
×	598
□	368
●	367
◆	934

Step 2: Backstitch (1 strand)

⌐	934

Step 1: Cross-stitch (2 strands)

DMC

✕	3045
○	223
□	326
+	340
■	333
●	924
∴	472
◆	934

Step 2: Backstitch (1 strand)

⌐	934

Victorian 93

Step 1: Cross-stitch (2 strands)

DMC

−	745
□	335
×	341
∴	334
+	926
▲	311
○	368
●	310

Step 2: Backstitch (1 stra

311

310

Step 3: French Knot (1 st

311

Step 1: Cross-stitch (2 strands)

DMC

−	744
╱	754
▲	3731
✕	340
△	747
○	958
●	991
+	3799

Step 2: Backstitch (1 strand)

⌐	3731
⌐	3799

Step 3: French Knot (1 strand)

⬤	3799

Step 1: Cross-stitch (2 strands)

DMC

	Ecru
○	754
✕	3326
■	210
∴	809
□	563
●	562
▲	420

Step 2: Backstitch (1 strand)

| ⌐ | 562 |
| ⌐ | 420 |

Step 1: Cross-stitch (2 strands)

DMC

- − 3770
- ○ 3078
- ∴ 899
- ✗ 3747
- △ 3325
- ▲ 826
- ✕ 964

Step 2: Backstitch (1 strand)

⌐ 3799

Step 3: French Knot (1 strand)

● 3799

Step 1: Cross-stitch (2 strands)

DMC

+	**3713**
●	**347**
✕	**3325**
○	**964**
□	**369**
■	**738**
◇	**839**

Step 2: Backstitch (1 strand)

⌐	**3799**

Step 3: French Knot (1 strand)

◆	**3799**

Step 1: Cross-stitch (2 strands)

DMC

	3713
o	3712
×	3731
●	327
∴	322
△	959
✗	3781
▲	310

Step 2: Backstitch (1 strand)

⌐ 310

Step 1: Cross-stitch (2 strands)

DMC

✎	725
–	352
□	554
∴	553
✕	959
○	964
●	501
▲	3371

Step 2: Backstitch (1 strand)

⌐	3371

100 Victorian ❧

Step 1: Cross-stitch (2 strands)

DMC

○	352
∴	3328
✕	340
△	3755
●	3760
–	964
▲	561

Step 2: Backstitch (1 strand)

⌐	3799

Step 1: Cross-stitch (2 strands)
DMC

▲ 725
○ 335
× 340
❘ 3761
● 3766
△ 989
╱ 986

Step 2: Backstitch (1 strand)

⌐ 3750

Step 1: Cross-stitch (2 strands)

DMC

–	3712
O	347
∴	327
✕	518
▲	517
☐	993
⁄	991

Step 2: Backstitch (1 strand)

⌐	3799

Step 1: Cross-stitch (2 strands)

DMC

I	760
●	347
×	341
□	327
○	368
■	367
△	3032

Step 2: Backstitch (1 strand)

⌐	3799

Step 1: Cross-stitch (2 strands)

DMC

		760
•		347
□		340
×		327
∕		368
■		367
·		3782

Step 2: Backstitch (1 strand)

⌐ 3799

Step 3: French Knot (1 strand)

◆ 3799

Step 3: French Knot (1 strand)

● 3031

Step 2: Backstitch (1 strand)

● 3031
✕ 414

⌐ 3031

◇ 3752
+ 930
□ 436
■ 632

Step 1: Cross-stitch (2 strands)

DMC

· 3770
○ 3779

Step 1: Cross-stitch (2 strands)

DMC

+	3047
△	676
○	353
✕	3712
∴	347
●	3752
╱	501
■	310

Step 2: Backstitch (1 strand)

⌐	310

Step 3: French Knot (1 strand)

✦	310

Victorian 107

Step 1: Cross-stitch (2 strands)
DMC

+	Ecru
∴	729
△	3779
○	3328
●	347
□	3345
✕	838

Step 2: Backstitch (1 strand)

⌐ 3371

Step 3: French Knot (1 strand)

◆ 3371

Step 1: Cross-stitch (2 strands)

DMC

+	950
○	352
●	208
□	519
■	517
×	3362
·	433

Step 2: Backstitch (1 strand)

⌐ 310

Step 3: French Knot (1 strand)

● 310

Step 1: Cross-stitch (2 strands)

DMC

∴	725
▲	351
–	3716
●	327
○	341
✁	322
☐	562
■	561

Step 2: Backstitch (1 strand)

┗ 561

Step 1: Cross-stitch (2 strands)

DMC

+	353
○	335
▲	326
✕	554
□	3766
■	806
△	3348
∴	3021

Step 2: Backstitch (1 strand)

⌐┘ 3021

Step 3: French Knot (1 strand)

● 3021

HOLIDAYS

Celebrate the joys of friendship, love, and happiness all the year through. Let every day be a holiday.

-Unknown

Step 1: Cross-stitch (2 strands)

DMC

+   **961**

○   **902**

□   **747**

✕   **792**

◇   **833**

◆   **3362**

■   **975**

●   **310**

Step 2: Backstitch (1 strand)

⌐   **310**

Step 3: French Knot (1 strand)

●   **310**

Step 1: Cross-stitch (2 strands)

DMC

+	729
○	3689
∴	3608
●	915
△	208
✕	996
■	319
□	310

Step 2: Backstitch (1 strand)

⌐   310

Step 3: French Knot (1 strand)

◆   310

Step 1: Cross-stitch (2 strands)

DMC

○	**676**
△	**3688**
▲	**3687**
−	**209**
✕	**340**
■	**993**
∴	**502**

Step 2: Backstitch (1 strand)

⌐	**3021**

Step 1: Cross-stitch (2 strands)

DMC

∴ 758

○ 961

+ 209

● 327

✕ 807

□ 502

▲ 840

Step 2: Backstitch (1 strand)

⌐ 3021

Step 3: French Knot (1 strand)

◆ 3021

Step 1: Cross-stitch (2 strands)

DMC

–	White
○	677
∴	676
▲	335
✕	208
⁄	799
●	987
△	632

Step 2: Backstitch (1 strand)

⌐	208
⌐	632

Step 3: French Knot (1 strand)

✦	632

Step 1: Cross-stitch (2 strands)

DMC

○	3340
●	900
✕	3350
■	702
+	738
△	436
∴	434
□	938

Step 2: Backstitch (1 strand)

⌐	702
⌐	434
⌐	938

Step 3: French Knot (1 strand)

◆	938

Step 1: Cross-stitch (2 strands)
DMC

- 676
O 963
∴ 961
△ 210
● 519
× 955
⁄ 840
▲ 938

Step 2: Backstitch (1 strand)

⌐ 938

Step 3: French Knot (1 strand)

✦ 938

Step 1: Cross-stitch (2 strands)

DMC

○   676
│   3778
●   326
△   210
∴   340
✦   958
□   840
▲   938

Step 2: Backstitch (1 strand)

└   938

Step 1: Cross-stitch (2 strands)

DMC

┃	**Ecru**
✕	**3731**
○	**816**
╱	**826**
∴	**824**
△	**436**
▲	**433**

Step 2: Backstitch (1 strand)

⌐	**3799**

Step 3: French Knot (1 strand)

●	**3799**

Step 1: Cross-stitch (2 strands)

DMC

△	**725**
☐	**335**
∴	**498**
I	**800**
○	**796**
✦	**700**
✕	**3032**
●	**310**

Step 2: Backstitch (1 strand)

⌐ **310**

Step 3: French Knot (1 strand)

✦ **310**

Step 1: Cross-stitch (2 strands)

DMC

+	Ecru
□	727
●	327
✕	702
·	470
○	436
◇	413
◆	310

Step 2: Backstitch (1 strand)

⌐	310

Step 3: French Knot (1 strand)

●	310

Step 1: Cross-stitch (2 strands)

DMC

		721
	△	720
	✕	747
	■	699
	∴	433
	○	413
	●	310

Step 2: Backstitch (1 strand)

⌐ 310

Step 3: French Knot (1 strand)

● 310

Step 1: Cross-stitch (2 strands)

DMC

·	712
○	721
△	959
∴	3345
✕	738
☐	436
●	869
■	3021

Step 2: Backstitch (1 strand)

⌐ 3021

Step 3: French Knot (1 strand)

✛ 3021

Step 1: Cross-stitch (2 strands)

DMC

❘	White	
✕	3607	
∴	498	
○	554	
▲	597	
△	704	
●	699	
⟋	310	

Step 2: Backstitch (1 strand)

⌐	310

Step 3: French Knot (1 strand)

◆	310

Step 1: Cross-stitch (2 strands)

DMC

○	3712
●	347
∴	498
□	369
✕	368
+	320
▲	319

Step 2: Backstitch (1 strand)

⌐	3799

Step 1: Cross-stitch (2 strands)

DMC

○	3712
●	347
∴	498
□	369
×	368
+	320
▲	319

Step 2: Backstitch (1 strand)

⌐	3799

Step 1: Cross-stitch (2 strands)

DMC

○	3712
●	347
∴	498
□	369
✕	368
+	320
▲	319

Step 2: Backstitch (1 strand)

⌐	3799

Step 1: Cross-stitch (2 strands)

DMC

I	778
○	347
✕	991
∴	738
△	434
□	3024
■	3787
●	3799

Step 2: Backstitch (1 strand)

⌐ 3799

Step 3: French Knot (1 strand)

✦ 3799

Step 1: Cross-stitch (2 strands)

DMC

•	White
○	962
∴	816
⁄	554
✕	552
●	955
☐	561

Step 2: Backstitch (1 strand)

⌐	310

Step 1: Cross-stitch (2 strands)

DMC

•	White
−	225
○	816
∴	554
●	3746
⁄	794
△	904
▲	310

Step 2: Backstitch (1 strand)

⌐	310

Step 3: French Knot (1 strand)

✦	310

Step 1: Cross-stitch (2 strands)

DMC

+	677
○	3328
●	347
□	813
■	825
✕	733
◇	890
·	435

Step 2: Backstitch (1 strand)

⌐	890

Step 3: French Knot (1 strand)

●	890

Step 2: Backstitch (1 strand)

⌐ 816
838

Step 3: French Knot (1 strand)

● 838

895
△ 3772
+ 838

Step 1: Cross-stitch (2 strands)

DMC

White
· 816
○ 327
■ 799
□ 798
●

Step 1: Cross-stitch (2 strands)

DMC

○	776
●	3350
△	3755
■	909
−	3774
∴	3772
▲	938

Step 2: Backstitch (1 strand)

   ⌐ 938

Step 1: Cross-stitch (2 strands)
DMC

△	White
○	351
✕	309
■	327
▣	813
∴	992
+	3362
●	839

Step 2: Backstitch (1 strand)

⌐	3362
⌐	839

Step 3: French Knot (1 strand)

●	3362

Step 1: Cross-stitch (2 strands)

DMC

✕	722
○	957
●	326
∴	553
△	799
╱	991
−	3772
▲	310

Step 2: Backstitch (1 strand)

└┐ 310

Step 3: French Knot (1 strand)

◆ 310

Step 1: Cross-stitch (2 strands)

DMC

·	677
+	3731
●	814
∴	327
×	826
		989
△	986
■	632

Step 2: Backstitch (1 strand)

⌐	826
⌐	632

#71 Right

Step 1: Cross-stitch (2 strands)

DMC

○	321
●	3746
✕	809
□	367
■	890
+	992
◇	407

Step 2: Backstitch (1 strand)

⌐	3799

CROSS-STITCH TIPS

FABRICS: Aida 14 is used for the samples of each design in this book. Counted cross-stitch is usually worked on even-weave fabric. These fabrics are manufactured specifically for counted-thread embroidery and are woven with the same number of vertical as horizontal threads per inch. Because the number of threads in the fabric is equal in each direction, each stitch will be the same size. It is the number of threads per inch in even-weave fabrics that determines the size of a finished design.

PREPARING FABRIC: Cut even-weave fabric at least 3" larger on all sides than the design size. A 3" margin is the minimum amount of space that allows for comfortably working the edges of the design. To prevent fraying, whipstitch or machine-zigzag raw fabric edges.

NEEDLES: Needles should slip easily through the holes in the fabric but not pierce the fabric. Use a blunt tapestry needle, size 24 or 26. Never leave the needle in the design area of your work. It can leave rust or a permanent impression on the fabric.

FLOSS: DMC brand floss is used for each design. Run the floss over a damp sponge to straighten. Separate all six strands and use the number of strands called for in the code.

CENTERING THE DESIGN: Fold the fabric in half horizontally, then vertically. Place a pin in the fold point to mark the center. Locate the center of the design on the graph by following the vertical and horizontal arrows in the left and bottom markings. Begin stitching all designs at the center point of the graph and the fabric.

GRAPHS: Each symbol represents a different color. Make one stitch for each symbol, referring to the code to verify which stitch to use.

CODES: The code indicates the brand of thread used to stitch the model. The steps in the code identify the stitch to be used and the number of floss strands for that stitch. The symbols match the graph, and give the color number for the thread.

SECURING THE FLOSS: Insert your needle up from the underside of the fabric at your starting point. Hold 1" of thread behind the fabric and stitch over it, securing it with the first few stitches. To finish the thread, run under four or more stitches on the back of the design. Never knot floss unless working on clothing. Another method of securing floss is the waste knot. Knot your floss and insert your needle from the right side o the fabric about 1" from the design area. Work several stitches over the thread to secure. Cut off the knot later.

STITCHING METHOD: For a smooth cross-stitch, use the "push-and-pull" method. Starting on wrong side of fabric, bring needle straight up, pulling floss completely through to right side. Re-insert needle and bring it back straight down, pulling needle and floss completely through to back of fabric. Keep floss flat but do not pull thread tight. Consistent tension throughout ensures even stitches. Make one stitch for every symbol on the chart. To stitch in rows, work from left to right and then back. Half-crosses are used to make a rounded shape. Make the longer stitch in the direction of the slanted line.

CARRYING FLOSS: To carry floss, weave floss under the previously worked stitches on the back. Do not carry thread across any fabric that is not or will not be stitched. Loose threads, especially dark ones, will show through the fabric.

CLEANING COMPLETED WORK: When stitching is complete, soak it in cold water with a mild soap for 5–10 minutes; rinse. Roll in a towel to remove excess water. Do not wring. Place work face down on a dry towel and iron on a warm setting until dry.

STITCHES

CROSS-STITCH: Make one cross-stitch for each symbol on chart. Bring needle up at A, down at B, up at C, down at D. For rows, stitch across fabric from left to right to make half-crosses and then back to complete stitches. All stitches should lie in the same direction.

BACKSTITCH: Complete all cross-stitching before working backstitches or other accent stitches. Working from left to right with one strand of floss (unless designated otherwise on code), bring needle and thread up at A, down at B, and up again at C. Go back down at A and continue in this manner.

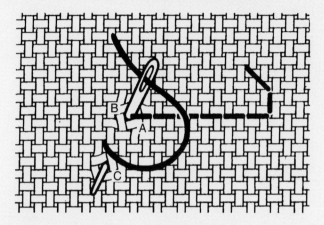

HALF-CROSS-STITCH: The stitch actually fits three-fourths of the area. Make the longer stitch in the direction of the slanted line on the graph. Bring needle and thread up at A, down at B, up at C, and down at D.

FRENCH KNOT: Bring the needle up at A, using one strand of embroidery floss. Wrap floss around needle two times. Insert needle beside A, pulling floss until it fits snugly around needle. Pull needle through to back.

METRIC EQUIVALENCE CHART

MM-Millimetres   CM-Centimetres

INCHES TO MILLIMETRES AND CENTIMETRES

INCHES	MM	CM	INCHES	CM	INCHES	CM
⅛	3	0.3	9	22.9	30	76.2
¼	6	0.6	10	25.4	31	78.7
½	13	1.3	12	30.5	33	83.8
⅝	16	1.6	13	33.0	34	86.4
¾	19	1.9	14	35.6	35	88.9
⅞	22	2.2	15	38.1	36	91.4
1	25	2.5	16	40.6	37	94.0
1¼	32	3.2	17	43.2	38	96.5
1½	38	3.8	18	45.7	39	99.1
1¾	44	4.4	19	48.3	40	101.6
2	51	5.1	20	50.8	41	104.1
2½	64	6.4	21	53.3	42	106.7
3	76	7.6	22	55.9	43	109.2
3½	89	8.9	23	58.4	44	111.8
4	102	10.2	24	61.0	45	114.3
4½	114	11.4	25	63.5	46	116.8
5	127	12.7	26	66.0	47	119.4
6	152	15.2	27	68.6	48	121.9
7	178	17.8	28	71.1	49	124.5
8	203	20.3	29	73.7	50	127.0

YARDS TO METRES

YARDS	METRES	YARDS	METRES	YARDS	METRES	YARDS	METRES	YARDS	METRES
⅛	0.11	2⅛	1.94	4⅛	3.77	6⅛	5.60	8⅛	7.43
¼	0.23	2¼	2.06	4¼	3.89	6¼	5.72	8¼	7.54
⅜	0.34	2⅜	2.17	4⅜	4.00	6⅜	5.83	8⅜	7.66
½	0.46	2½	2.29	4½	4.11	6½	5.94	8½	7.77
⅝	0.57	2⅝	2.40	4⅝	4.23	6⅝	6.06	8⅝	7.89
¾	0.69	2¾	2.51	4¾	4.34	6¾	6.17	8¾	8.00
⅞	0.80	2⅞	2.63	4⅞	4.46	6⅞	6.29	8⅞	8.12
1	0.91	3	2.74	5	4.57	7	6.40	9	8.23
1⅛	1.03	3⅛	2.86	5⅛	4.69	7⅛	6.52	9⅛	8.34
1¼	1.14	3¼	2.97	5¼	4.80	7¼	6.63	9¼	8.46
1⅜	1.26	3⅜	3.09	5⅜	4.91	7⅜	6.74	9⅜	8.57
1½	1.37	3½	3.20	5½	5.03	7½	6.86	9½	8.69
1⅝	1.49	3⅝	3.31	5⅝	5.14	7⅝	6.97	9⅝	8.80
1¾	1.60	3¾	3.43	5¾	5.26	7¾	7.09	9¾	8.92
1⅞	1.71	3⅞	3.54	5⅞	5.37	7⅞	7.20	9⅞	9.03
2	1.83	4	3.66	6	5.49	8	7.32	10	9.14

INDEX